IT'S TIME TO EAT CHOCOLATE WAFFLE COOKIES

It's Time to Eat CHOCOLATE WAFFLE COOKIES

Walter the Educator

Silent King Books
A WhichHead Entertainment Imprint

Copyright © 2024 by Walter the Educator

All rights reserved. No part of this book may be reproduced in any manner whatsoever without written per- mission except in the case of brief quotations embodied in critical articles and reviews.

First Printing, 2024

Disclaimer

This book is a literary work; the story is not about specific persons, locations, situations, and/or circumstances unless mentioned in a historical context. Any resemblance to real persons, locations, situations, and/or circumstances is coincidental. This book is for entertainment and informational purposes only. The author and publisher offer this information without warranties expressed or implied. No matter the grounds, neither the author nor the publisher will be accountable for any losses, injuries, or other damages caused by the reader's use of this book. The use of this book acknowledges an understanding and acceptance of this disclaimer.

It's Time to Eat CHOCOLATE WAFFLE COOKIES is a collectible early learning book by Walter the Educator suitable for all ages belonging to Walter the Educator's Time to Eat Book Series. Collect more books at WaltertheEducator.com

USE THE EXTRA SPACE TO TAKE NOTES AND DOCUMENT YOUR MEMORIES

CHOCOLATE WAFFLE COOKIES

It's time, it's time, to have a treat,

It's Time to Eat

Chocolate Waffle Cookies

A yummy snack that can't be beat!

Chocolate waffle cookies, oh so sweet,

Let's gather 'round, it's time to eat!

The waffles are crisp, the chocolate's warm,

Together they make the perfect charm.

With every bite, we giggle and cheer,

Chocolate waffles are here, my dear!

Sprinkles and frosting, what a delight,

The cookies are shining in the light.

Take a big bite, don't be shy,

Chocolate waffle cookies, oh my, oh my!

Crunchy, soft, and full of fun,

We'll eat them all, there's so much to munch!

One for you and one for me,

Let's share our cookies, joyfully!

It's Time to Eat Chocolate Waffle Cookies

Round and round, they fit just right,

Baked to perfection, a sweet delight.

The chocolate melts with every chew,

The waffle makes it perfect too!

Melted gooey goodness inside,

It's the best treat, no need to hide.

Take a cookie, have a bite,

Chocolate waffles, day or night!

We dunk them in milk, it's so much fun,

One cookie, two cookies, three, then done!

The taste is magic, it's true,

Chocolate waffle cookies, yum, who knew?

They're warm, they're cool, they're just so neat,

A perfect snack when we meet.

Let's enjoy each crunchy crumb,

It's Time to Eat
Chocolate Waffle Cookies

Chocolate waffles are second to none!

Time to eat, the table's set,

Chocolate waffle cookies, the best treat yet!

Take your plate, take your spoon,

Chocolate waffles, oh, so soon!

Now we're done, but wait, don't fear!

Chocolate waffle cookies will always be near!

We'll make them again, next time to share,

It's Time to Eat
Chocolate Waffle Cookies

A cookie party beyond compare!

ABOUT THE CREATOR

Walter the Educator is one of the pseudonyms for Walter Anderson. Formally educated in Chemistry, Business, and Education, he is an educator, an author, a diverse entrepreneur, and he is the son of a disabled war veteran. "Walter the Educator" shares his time between educating and creating. He holds interests and owns several creative projects that entertain, enlighten, enhance, and educate, hoping to inspire and motivate you. Follow, find new works, and stay up to date with Walter the Educator™

at WaltertheEducator.com

www.ingramcontent.com/pod-product-compliance
Lightning Source LLC
LaVergne TN
LVHW052011060526
838201LV00059B/3969